Mataus and Marius

Written and Photographed by:

Diane Baxter Trapeni

Keep an eye out for these other exciting titles:

Nellie the Nibbler

Alice the Guinea Pig

Penny the Python

Jeremiah, a Song Bird

Vincent (Christmas reindeer)

Hubert

Phil Harmonic

Jeff Sticks up for his Buddies

Cord, Glue and 8 Screws

Sydney Has Friends

DEDICATION

To Ken's daughter, Cameron, who is one of the
lights of his life!   DMBT

Mataus misses his little brother, Marius. They've always been together...until NOW! Mataus needs a plan to get his brother to come home. (Last Sunday Marius took off for the Big City.)

Their argument was over the giant anthill on Colonel Haverty's land. It was so silly. There were enough ants for both of them!

For now, Mataus didn't know what to do. He was depressed, so he ate. He ate 30,000 ants in one day! Ants for breakfast... ants for lunch... and ants for dinner!

He spent so much time eating that he began

to really look at his food.

The ants were very organized.

They were very interesting.   They could

design, build, hunt, and make tunnels all

with precision-like coordination!

Mataus was very impressed indeed.   He even dreamed about them and this is what he came up with...His big "AhHa momentl"

He saw the ants encased in a clear, glass or plastic like the bees & beetles were for necklaces, key chains, brooches, bracelets, rings and hairpieces!
He awoke with a start.

"That's it!" he yelled out loud. "I know how I can get Marius back!!!"

Mataus sent a picture to Marius with samples of his ideas. Marius and Mataus' Bug Jool Designs was what he called his new business adventure.

Mataus began to get more and more excited. WOW, how about buggy belts for the boys and bugs on cowboy hats (Kinky Skink will want one!). This idea of making ants and bugs jools was almost more exciting than eating them.Almost!

The brothers could pay off all their bills. They could work together every day. They'd get momma a new home.

They could donate to their favorite charity, "Save the Sloths". (Stanley Sloth is their poor relation, you know!)

Marius' thoughts:

"I am Mataus' little brother so I, too, am an anteater. We had a little disagreement and I left home. I hate the city but here I am. I really want to go home."

(Can you spot Officer Green?)

Marius just received his brother's letter. It sounded wonderful. Like a gift, it was a reason to go home!

He wanted to be a part of it!

He missed his momma a lot.

Marius wasn't even upset anymore. They would forgive and they already forgot! He jumped on the bus and within 2 hours, he was HOME.

Together they drew many designs. They added to the line of jools with yellow wasp brooches, mosquito pins for red bomber jackets, beetle keychains and necklaces and made lots of money!

Mataus threw his arms around his little brother's shoulders and announced that the company would be led by him. "Let's get started little brother. You're the boss!"

The End

(of breaking up over the little things)

Keep an eye out for these other exciting Children's Books:

Dot and Comma with Friends

Floyd the Colorful Chameleon

Francesca the Tropical Red-eyed Green Frog

Joe's Got Spots

Merrill the Squirrel and Jen the Hen:

Part 6 Brittany's Back!!!

Christmas at the Mountain Top Inn and Resort

A Three Piggie Circus

Frances, a Gifted Frog for Sure!

Saffire. (Butterfly)

Serendipity. (Fish)

Big Louie's Dead (But not Forgotten)

Christmas at the Castle

We are proud to introduce:

Genevieve, and the Case of the Missing Apple

Genevieve always wanted to help others so she became a Private Investigator. Her first case was back at school. Someone was stealing Mrs. Nelson's apple every day!!! Mrs. Nelson called on Genny to solve the mystery. You won't believe who dunnit and why?

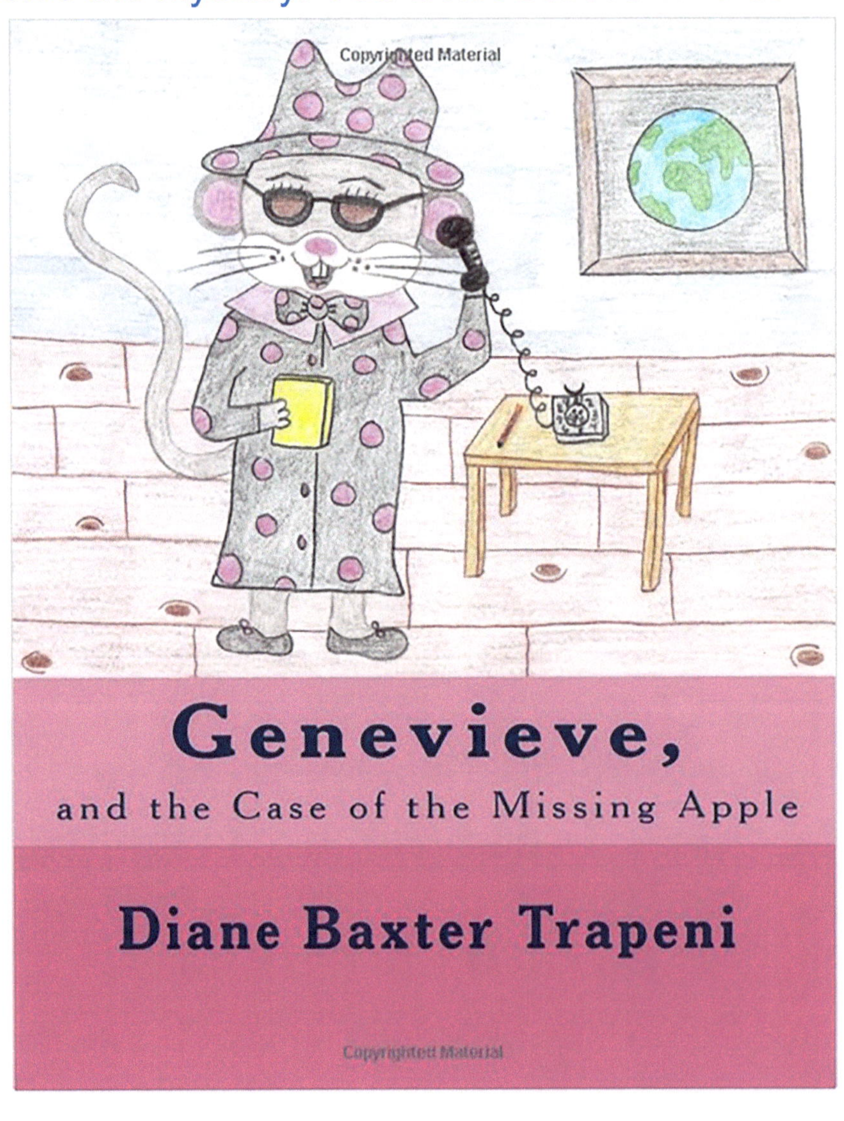

About the TrapStone LLC: Owner and Author…

My name is Miss Diane. I taught for 42

years and have read thousands of books

aloud to children.

I enjoyed that so much, I decided to write

and illustrate books for you myself.

Enjoy!!!

About the TrapStone LLC: Manager…

Ken Stone Sr. is a computer programmer and a business partner extraordinaire. He put my words, pictures and computer magic together so you could meet… Mataus and Marius.